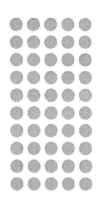

S0-BHG-180

50
TIPS FOR EFFECTIVE NETWORKING

by Mark Mikelat
Building Aspirations

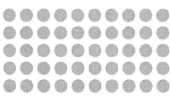

50 Tips for Effective Networking
by Mark Mikelat

Book Designers:
Paula Chance and Betsy Carman,
mudpie graphics, inc.

For more information, contact:
Mark Mikelat
PO Box 14885
Long Beach, CA 90803

mark@buildingaspirations.com

Buildingaspirations.com

ISBN: 978-1-934468-00-5
Library of Congress Catalog Number in Publication Data

Printed in the United States of America

TABLE OF CONTENTS

Introduction . . . . page 5

Chapter 1 | Your Networking Strategy . . . . . . page 7

Chapter 2 | Relationship Building . . . . .page 18

Chapter 3 | Personal Communication . . . . . .page 29

Chapter 4 | Personal Image . . . . page 40

Chapter 5 | Event Management . . . . page 51

To Learn More . . . . page 63

About the Author . . . . page 64

INTRODUCTION

Professional networking is a simple yet powerful idea. We are all connected to each other through other people. In the media and everyday speech this idea is referred to in various ways:

Six-degrees of separation.
You need to know somebody.
It's not, what you know. It's who you know.

This book provides basic tips to help you more effectively benefit from your networking.

The tips in this book are organized into five broad categories. Chapter 1, Your Networking Strategy, helps you create a good plan. In Chapter 2, Relationship Building, we emphasize the power of a personal relationship. Chapter 3, Personal Communication, lists tips for more effective communication while networking. Next, in Chapter 4, Personal Image,

I emphasize the need to manage yourself as a brand. Finally, Chapter 5, Event Management, offers tips on types of networking events.

Have a good read. And keep networking!

Chapter 1

YOUR NETWORKING STRATEGY

The majority of men meet with failure because of their lack of persistence in creating new plans to take the place of those which fail.

—Napoleon Hill

Tip 1
HAVE NETWORKING GOALS.

Know what you want to achieve from your networking experience. Your goal is to *network*, but what does that mean? Do you want to meet just one good-quality person? Do you want to meet everyone in the room? Do you want to meet potential clients, business partners, or people who can hire you?

What do you want out of that engagement? Having goals enables you to use your time and energy more effectively. If you want to meet only one high-quality person for example, then once you find a person with whom you can connect, you know that you can spend the rest of the evening with that one person. Because you've accomplished your goal, you can comfortably give the person you've met your undivided attention to learn about them, their business, and what they want.

A focused goal might be, "I need to find somebody today who is knowledgeable about e-mail marketing." By setting goals at the outset, you can be more effective in your networking efforts.

Tip ❷
HAVE A NETWORKING SYSTEM.

The building blocks of a good system center around the basic questions, When, Where, Why, How, and Who.

When are you most available for networking? For example, what is better for your schedule? Weekend conferences? Evening mixers?

Where can you best invest your time? Perhaps you have a specific geographic area where you're most comfortable.

Why should you be networking? Do you want to grow your business? Learn from others? Find a different job?

How do you intend to network? Will you attend small weekly meetings? Large conferences? Informal one-on-one sessions?

Who(m) do you wish to connect with? Perhaps you are seeking people in a specific industry, such as consumer products.

Having a networking system allows you to leverage your networking goal (Tip 1) for the greatest effectiveness.

Tip 3
HAVE A FOLLOW-UP SYSTEM.

With the first three tips, we are seeking to get you organized in your networking efforts. Networking is about building relationships with people, an idea that is strong enough to warrant more in-depth discussion in Chapter 3. In order to connect with people and have them know you, you must *first know them*. This starts with keeping in touch with them. You need to develop a system for following up with people.

Why do you need a follow-up system? It is extremely unlikely that you'll meet a person at a networking event, exchange business cards, and immediately form a professional relationship. There needs to be an opportunity for courtship. You need to get to know each other. Your first step is following up with them.

Determine the method that is most effective for you. Perhaps you can call people you meet once a month or send them press releases from your company. Only by keeping in touch with people can you hope to nurture mutually beneficial and rewarding professional relationships.

Tip ④
NETWORK BEFORE YOU NEED TO.

Realize that the best time to network is *right now*. Oftentimes, people misunderstand the value of networking and only begin to work on it when there is a pending need, such as a sales campaign or a job transition.

Always remember that your professional network is not just about you. You should help people and they should help you. If you wait for the specific time when you *need* something, you are doing a disservice to people. By adapting an attitude of persistent and constant networking, you will always provide yourself an opportunity to help others and for others to help you.

Responding to needs is a very reactive strategy. When you build an effective professional network, you can create opportunities. This proactive strategy is far more effective and rewarding than merely reacting. Until immediate needs present themselves, you can work to develop opportunities. As needs arise, such as a sales campaign or job transition, you can more effectively and immediately address them.

Tip ⑤
NETWORK EVERYWHERE.

You do not have to network only at networking events. There are opportunities everywhere. For example, I once attended a career workshop and heard the following story about good networking.

A man who had recently been terminated by the board of directors of a telecommunications firm was traveling in a taxi. He had been the firm's CEO. As taxi drivers do, his driver just started chatting with his fare and learned the passenger's situation. The taxi driver's brother had founded a start-up telecommunications company and had recently entered an expansion phase with an infusion of capital from a venture capital firm.

The brother's telecommunications enterprise needed a proven CEO to lead the company. Here he was! He was sitting in the back of the cab. The passenger contacted the company's founder, learned their mission, and went in for an interview. The firm eventually hired him.

You never know where and when networking opportunities can appear. You can network anywhere, even if you are a corporate executive sitting in the back of a taxi cab.

Tip ❻
GREET A NEW PERSON IMMEDIATELY UPON ARRIVING AT AN EVENT.

Sometimes when you are approaching an event, especially an unfamiliar event, you feel awkward or nervous. We are naturally apprehensive with new surroundings. At such times, it is helpful to break the ice. You can do this, and relieve your nervousness, by greeting somebody as soon as you get to the event.

If you break the ice immediately, you prove to yourself that it is easier than you had anticipated. A successful introduction and conversation with a person you may have never spoken to before creates encouragement to help you continue networking.

People are often intimidated by their apprehension, fear, and awkwardness in the face of the task of speaking to people who may be total strangers. They fail to realize that, more often than not, almost everyone else at the event is feeling the same trepidations. Not only will you be helping yourself, but you will also be helping the other person you talk to. You'll help them address their own nervousness and fear.

Tip ❼
DON'T BE A COMPLAINER.

Sure, we all need to vent our anger sometimes. But a networking event may not be the proper place. Imagine this scenario. You've pre-registered for an event and developed your networking plan. You are excited about attending this event. But you've already put in a full day of work. The minute you arrive at the event, you encounter somebody who proceeds to complain to you about all of his or her personal challenges.

This may be your very first meeting with this person. What do you remember about them? Do you think that they want to be remembered for the challenge that they had fixing their car or their broken-down copy machine at work? To mention a negative issue in passing as a part of normal conversation is one thing, but having it be the center of your conversation is quite another. Complaining is negative conversation. You want your networking to be a positive experience.

You are working to be remembered. Do you want to be remembered as a complainer? I suspect that is not the lasting impression you want to make. You want to be remembered for being a positive person.

Tip ❽
BE A GIVER, NOT A TAKER.

We most easily get something when we give something away. People are naturally apprehensive and defensive when we ask them for things as soon as we meet them. The following are examples of people concentrating on *taking*:

When can I come your office?
When can I call you?
When can we talk about you buying my product?

These questions are too aggressive for a networking session, especially a first meeting. You need to engage in networking with a philosophy of *giving* to people. The following are good giving examples:

I've some great referrals that I can give you.
Would you be interested in a free demonstration?
I have some samples that I can give you.

Effective networking is not self-centered. As you help more people, more people will help you. Givers are rewarded.

Tip 9
GREET YOUR FRIENDS, BUT DON'T SPEND ALL YOUR TIME WITH THEM.

Many times when I'm speaking with and getting to know a new person, they walk away, saying, "Excuse me, I see somebody I know." Of course, you want to say hello to people you know. At a networking mixer, however, you want to meet new people.

I've witnessed this example of ineffective networking too often. It is especially comical to see it in action at a luncheon mixer. People will sit at a table with their co-workers and colleagues. If you work with these people, you see them every workday. You already know them. One of the general purposes of a networking event is to meet new people. It is far easier to accomplish this goal if you sit with people you don't already know.

If you spend time with people you already know, you are missing an opportunity. You are not taking advantage of the opportunity to meet and connect with people you don't already know. Be focused on spending the majority of the time meeting new people, not conversing with old friends.

Tip ⑩
DON'T DRINK EXCESSIVELY.

As part of your networking strategy, you are branding yourself. You are creating a personal image. People who drink excessively broadcast an unprofessional image.

In some circumstances, it may be challenging not to drink too much. Some large mixers, trade shows, and corporate parties feature open bars. Although this is a social part of a personal networking experience, you must remember to present a positive image.

You want to make a positive impression on people. They should remember you, your product, your personal image, your brand. You don't want them to remember your alcohol-induced slurred speech or obnoxious attitude.

If alcohol represents any risk for you, avoid it. There is no reason that you can't have a soda or a glass of water at a professional mixer when everyone else is drinking wine. These days, sobriety is perfectly acceptable. It does not look unusual. You need to project a positive and professional image to an event's attendees. Don't sabotage yourself by drinking too much.

Chapter 2

RELATIONSHIP BUILDING

Don't judge each day by the harvest you reap but by the seeds that you plant.

—Robert Louis Stevenson

Tip ⓫
LEARN THEIR BUSINESS.

When you meet somebody new, learn his or her business. You cannot easily evaluate whether or not a business can use you or your product or service until you first understand that business.

You can ask the person you meet what they do and how long they have been in business. It is far easier to build a professional relationship with somebody when you have a good understanding of his or her business.

I was participating in a networking mixer a short time ago when an attendee pitched his product to me by saying, "Mark, you need this." But he had no way of knowing what I might need without knowing my business. His assumption was self-centric and focused on his own business, not on mine. Maybe I already had his product. He hadn't asked and he didn't know.

You can only learn about the needs of other people by investing the time and effort to learn about their business. A sales strategy without this basic step is ineffective. It is overly aggressive and will eventually result in people avoiding you. Know the other person's business.

Tip ⑫
REMEMBER PEOPLE'S NAMES.

One of the most powerful ways to show respect for an individual is to remember their name. The skill of remembering names is a difficult one to master, but it is well worth the time and effort.

In professional networking situations, you'll have props to help you hone this skill. At mixers, for example, people will often be wearing a name badge. Try to associate their name with something unique and distinctive about them. When you meet them in another situation, the fact that you can quickly remember their name will leave a long-lasting positive impression.

The more time and effort you devote to mastering this skill, the easier it will be to remember more names in the future. When you can greet an individual by name without an introduction, that makes that person feel more appreciated. Who would you rather work with—someone who took the time and energy to learn and remember your name or somebody who muttered, "What was your name again?"

Tip ⓭
BE HONEST.

People want honesty in the people with whom they work. In the business world, we are too often over-promised and under-satisfied. Hyperbolism in the form of empty promises abounds in the marketing and advertising messages that saturate our daily lives. Do not over-exaggerate or indulge in hyperbole when you network. Don't misrepresent yourself or your business.

I remember a comment that a consultant made to me over a networking breakfast meeting. As I pitched a potential client to her, she replied that the client wasn't a good fit for her marketing strategy consulting firm. The consulting practice I was trying to recommend didn't have enough expertise in the client's specific area.

Her candor was refreshing. She was being totally honest with me. I appreciated that. Other people might have presented their firm's experience in a way to convince me that it was the perfect business partner. But she didn't do this. Her honesty resonated with me and thus made her more memorable. Thanks to her honesty, I'll continue to keep her in mind for future potential opportunities.

SHOW INTEREST IN PEOPLE BY ASKING SINCERE QUESTIONS.

People love to talk. More specifically, they love to talk about their favorite subject: themselves. Let them. Encourage them by asking questions. It's critical, however, that you ask *sincere* questions.

Here's an example of an insincere question. At a trade show, a sales person for data storage service once asked me, "Which provider does your client use?" This is an insincere question. The sales rep didn't really care about my client's needs. He was doing a competitive analysis in the hope of winning new business. He was focused not on the client, but rather himself and his need to make a sale.

You need to build a relationship first. Then ask for the sale.

A more sincere question, like "Can your client manage all of its data effectively?" demonstrates interest in the needs of the firm. Show sincere interest in the other person. By sincerely listening to people, you reinforce your goal of relationship building.

Tip ⑮
BE RESPECTFUL OF PEOPLE.

When you think of practicing courteous and respectful behavior, use the Golden Rule as your guideline.

Treat others like you would like to be treated.

People remember disrespectful behavior more vividly than respectful behavior. Worse yet, they are more likely to share these negative experiences with others. If this lack of respect is associated with you or your company, you're creating an impediment to effective relationship building.

At one point in my career I learned of a not-for-profit organization seeking volunteer workshop leaders to teach personal development workshops to the recently retired. I called a contact I found on their website. The woman I called, who was not the volunteer co-coordinator, became angry with me. She was not the proper person to speak with and she berated me for having called her. They lost an opportunity. Her disrespect killed my motivation to volunteer and hence they lost an opportunity to have an experienced workshop leader help their organization.

Tip 16
GIVE YOUR FULL ATTENTION TO THE PERSON YOU'RE SPEAKING TO.

When you are speaking to someone, pay attention to him or her. Life is full of distractions. Work to avoid this by focusing on your conversational partner. When you're giving them your full attention, you'll more easily hear and understand what they have to say.

Make eye contact with people when you're speaking with them. Human behavioral studies have documented the fact that eye contact with another person makes verbal communication both more positive and more effective.

Let me point out that speaking over the phone doesn't excuse you from practicing this simple skill of giving people your attention. I've experienced people being distracted by e-mail while we're talking on the phone. Be aware that if we're on a call with someone while we're reading, or worse yet, typing an e-mail, we can't concentrate on the phone conversation. By providing your full attention, you'll show respect to the other person while being a more effective communicator.

Tip ⑰
BE A LISTENER, NOT A TALKER.

The most effective communicators are those who listen more than they speak. It's an old but true saying that people have two ears and one mouth. That should serve as a simple reminder to listen twice as much as you speak. To better understand a person's issue, you need to actively listen to them.

I once had a manager who truly excelled as an effective communicator. Part of his strength grew from the fact that he rarely spoke. Our department would have lengthy and involved strategy sessions with several critical topics being discussed back and forth. Everyone in the room would be talking. He would be listening.

After politely listening to all of his subordinates, he was able to organize the information and focus on the most important issues. He might speak only a few words, but his words were usually the most valuable comments made in the entire meeting. We become better at talking with people when we first listen to them.

Tip ⑱
ASK CREATIVE AND OPEN-ENDED QUESTIONS.

Conversations at networking mixers are sometimes troublesome. Two strangers starting a conversation with one another might stumble over what to talk about. You can address this challenge by being more creative with open-ended questions.

The standard question, "What do you do?", inspires yawns in people familiar with networking. This question is old, tired, and boring. At large functions, you'll hear it being asked all over the room. To stand out as a networker, find a more creative and distinctive way to ask questions. People will appreciate you taking the time to be more creative.

If you're at a marketing event try something like this:

"How do you think marketers can most effectively target the 18-25-year-old segment?"

This kind of question will get a conversation started and you'll have a greater opportunity to learn more about the person's marketing skills and experience. Creative questions build creative conversations.

Tip ⑲
REWARD REFERRALS.

If somebody gives you a good referral, show your appreciation with a reward. If you get a good contact or a lead that results in a sale, reward the person who gave you the referral. That is only kind and considerate. I encourage you to reward other referrals as well. You can benefit significantly if you find an excellent business partner or a potential employee via a personal referral. That type of referral deserves recognition as well.

Generally, when people are giving referrals, they are not seeking compensation, but rather recognition and a show of appreciation. Your reward does not always need to be financial. The reward could take the form of a simple card or a sincere thank-you phone call.

The type of reward is your choice. It really depends on the type of referral and its value or the resultant benefit. Make sure that the reward is appropriate. If you don't know the person who referred you very well, a dinner invitation may be inappropriate while sending them a nice gift certificate might be fine.

Tip ⑳
FIND THINGS IN COMMON WITH PEOPLE.

People connect more easily with people when they can find common ground. When we seek to form a professional relationship with people, we need to be like-minded in some things. These commonalities can be personal or professional. Work to find this common ground.

Sometimes commonality may be already established at a networking event. People attending a mixer generally have a common professional link. If you're attending a mixer for meeting planners for example, you can share stories about the challenges of managing hotel contracts or a late registration process. Because your colleagues are likely to have some degree of experience with these issues, they'll have a higher level of appreciation for your anecdotes.

People feel better, safer, and more comfortable with familiar things, and this includes topics of conversation. If you're at a marketing conference, talk about marketing. If you concentrate on common topics, people can more easily understand you and connect more easily with you and what you are saying.

Chapter 3

PERSONAL COMMUNICATION

Good communication is as stimulating as black coffee and just as hard to sleep after.

—Anne Morrow Lindbergh

Tip ㉑
HAVE A FIRM HANDSHAKE.

I t is very important to have an immediate positive connection with another person. In a professional networking situation, you can accomplish this partly with a firm handshake. Some people think that it's trite or stereotypical, but it has actually been re-searched and documented that in the United States a firm handshake does have a positive impact. Both men and women should have firm handshakes.

Let's walk through a quick lesson in shaking hands properly. Put your right hand out, directly toward the person you're greeting. When you extend a hand, it should be relatively unbent and firm. Grasp the other person's hand with one hand, not both, and shake it two or three times, firmly, but not vigorously. If your grip is too soft, you'll seem uncommitted; if it's too firm, you'll seem aggressive. While you are shaking the person's hand, look them in the eye and greet them by name.

If you come from a culture that bows or kisses as part of your general greeting, a firm handshake may seem awkward at first, but rest assured that it is an impor-tant part of effective networking.

Tip ㉒
WEAR A NAME TAG.

Usually when we go to a professional networking meeting, our name tag will be waiting for us, especially if there's some registration process. Generally they will have your first and last name and your company name.

See your name tag as your marketing billboard. Take advantage of the format of the name tag. For example, do you want to use only your first name, or do you want to use both first and last names? Do you want your company name to come first? Sometimes this registration process happens via a web page so you can enter the information as you see most appropriate. A name tag template may say first name, but that doesn't mean that you cannot enter the company name if you really want your company name to be first on your name tag.

This is an integral part of your strategy to effectively communicate your message. To be more creative and original, you can even go to a local engraver and have a relatively inexpensive brass name tag made.

Tip ㉓
MAKE A BRAND OF YOURSELF.

By making a brand of yourself, you make yourself more memorable. You want to be remembered for your company and your product. For example, if you're a real estate professional and go to a significantly large, general networking event, there will be multiple real estate professionals. So how do you stand out among your peers?

You don't want to be remembered vaguely:

"Oh, I think he works in real estate somewhere."

You want people to understand and remember your brand:

"He's a real estate lender at ABC Loans in Los Angeles."

Branding is powerful. For example, people associate Disney with its products and services—movies, amusement parks, and family-themed entertainment. You want people to just as effortlessly remember you and your message. If your company is XYZ Corporation, you need to create a way for people to remember that brand and accurately associate it with you.

Tip ㉔
HAVE A 30-SECOND COMMERCIAL.

Because people have short attention spans and they are easily confused and distracted, you need to be able to introduce yourself and explain who you are in a few words. A quick, concise personal commercial helps people focus on you.

Lack of focus is particularly difficult for people networking while they are in job transition. When speaking to you, job seekers may go on and on for two or three minutes about their former jobs, but they never tell you what type of job they're seeking. A person only has a few seconds to make a positive impression. Make the impression.

Which is the more effective personal commercial?

"I'm a professional advertising executive seeking senior-level management opportunities in the consumer products industry."

"I'm looking for a job."

You need to tell people what you want. Use your 30-second commercial to accomplish this.

KEEP IN TOUCH WITH PEOPLE.

Networking doesn't end with the end of the networking event. People give you their contact information for a reason. I explained the value of a follow-up system in Chapter 1. A great system only works when you actually use it. Keep in touch with people by implementing your follow-up system.

People want to maintain contact with you. Sometimes opportunities develop because you've kept in touch. People hear of something you need to know and remember you. This has happened to me countless times. I might contact an associate with whom I've not worked for a while just to see up how they're doing. They might contact me a couple of weeks later when a new opportunity comes across their desk.

Just recently, for example, I had lunch with a colleague who has been growing his computer consulting business. He really wanted to take it to another level for greater sales and expansion. Over lunch we talked about how I could be a spokesperson for some of his products. Had I not kept in touch with this person, this mutually beneficial opportunity would never have developed.

Tip ㉖
HAVE A CONVERSATIONAL PROP.

The art of conversation is a tough skill to master. Some of us just don't always know what to say. You can help yourself by carrying a prop at networking events. This might be a product you're selling or a book you wrote. This prop is not only a safe and non-threatening way to break the conversational ice, but it also makes you more memorable to those you meet.

The best prop is a physical, tangible object. People understand and remember it. Pick something that is consistent with and reinforces your brand. If you're a professional photographer, for example, carry a camera.

This strategy is particularly effective because it's so seldom used. Imagine hundreds of people at a mixer, and you're the only one with a bag of product samples. You're unique. You'll be remembered.

But don't carry a prop that is silly or whimsical. You should be focused on being creative, and memorable, but most of all, you want to be perceived as professional. If your prop is inappropriate, it will hinder your efforts to communicate more effectively.

Tip㉗
POSITIVE-POSITION YOUR MESSAGE.

Take the best information you have and present it in the best possible way. This is a personal public relations strategy. Now, I'm not advocating lying in any way, shape, or form. I oppose lying. Take the information you have, carefully select the best words, and present it as best you can.

You are not *unemployed.* You are in a *job transition.* You are not *laid-off.* You're *seeking new opportunities.*

If your company went bankrupt, you don't need to mention that. If it comes up in conversation, you may certainly talk about it, but remember—you're working to communicate a positive message. Giving negative information early on in a conversation with a new person might make them associate you with this negative circumstance.

If you want a contact to remember one thing about you, do you want them to remember "Web-marketing guru" or "The guy from the bankrupt company"? Present your information in the best possible light.

Tip ㉘
MAKE SURE YOUR BUSINESS CARD IS ACCURATE.

Your business card is your most basic marketing tool. It must give your correct address and other contact information. You can only communicate effectively with accurate information. Time and time again, I've encountered people who fail to appreciate this. People have given me their business card and immediately said, "But that information is wrong, though."

Have you ever purposely put an incorrect address on a letter and then mailed it? Do you ever drive somewhere but drive in the wrong direction on purpose? Of course you don't do any of these things. Don't have wrong information on your business card.

Mistakes happen, but this is different than knowingly having wrong information. If you have out-dated information have new business cards printed. The time and expense you devote to this marketing investment is minor.

Your business card communicates your message. Make sure it's accurate. Incorrect information not only sends a negative message but it also makes follow-up more difficult.

Tip ㉙
BE CONCISE AND SPECIFIC.

In a networking situation you have a limited amount of time with a person, which means you need to speak concisely and specifically. People cannot help you if you cannot, in very specific terms, tell them what you want.

At a recent career development workshop I was trying to coach a young man into telling me what he wanted in a career. I had brought my collection of business cards and was ready to offer phone numbers of people for him to call.

But the student had difficulty articulating his career aspiration. He couldn't speak clearly about what he wanted. There was a stack of good potential contacts on the table right in front of him, but I needed to know what to look for before I could hand him a specific card. The cards represented a wide range of "interesting" and "challenging" careers, the only phrases this young man could think of. I needed a concise and specific idea of what kind of job he wanted. Only then would I know what kind of contact to give him.

Tip ㉚
ASK PEOPLE TO INTRODUCE YOU TO OTHER PEOPLE.

We are all linked together via a short chain of relationships. You can build your chain by asking people you know to introduce you to people they know.

Imagine that you started with one person and asked her to introduce you to two people. You then asked these two people to each introduce you to two people. If you did that ten times, how many people would you meet?

$(2*2*2*2*2*2*2*2*2*2)$ or $2^{10}=1024$ people. You can be introduced to 1024 people with the simple question: "Could you introduce me to two people you know?"

You can easily use this method at a networking mixer. It might be an especially valuable strategy if you are more inhibited about meeting people on your own. If an individual escorts you to somebody she knows and introduces you, you've just received an informal personal testimonial. Even upon the first introduction, you are not seen as a stranger, but rather somebody that so-and-so already knows.

Chapter 4

PERSONAL IMAGE

Real integrity is doing the right thing, knowing that nobody's going to know whether you did it or not.

—Oprah Winfrey

Tip ㉛
BE MEMORABLE.

You are creating your personal brand, or personal image; you do that by being memorable. Sometimes people forget this simple idea. You might be more experienced, more skillful, and have a better product than somebody else, but if your potential buyer doesn't remember who you are, then all those superior qualities really don't matter.

You must be remembered in a *positive* way. You do not want to be remembered for being loud and obnoxious, for vulgar speech or poor dress or poor attitude. You want to be remembered for admirable qualities—for being professional, smart, and energetic.

In the college courses I teach, I'm always preaching the idea of professional networking to my students. My students have unique opportunities to make themselves memorable. By seeking out business professionals, meeting them, and getting to know them, they become memorable to their future potential employers. When it comes time to hire people, managers can review a stack of resumes of anonymous candidates, or they can call an impressive student they remember.

Tip ㉜
BE PROFESSIONALLY DRESSED.

A picture is worth a thousand words, and the way you dress is your picture. People draw inferences about you from your mode of dress. To present yourself in the best image, dress professionally.

Note that this is not merely an adage for the business world. A colleague of mine who owns several fast food restaurants has shared stories about his employees' lack of professional dress. Far too often, he says, candidates for jobs would show up dressed in a T-shirt and jeans. No matter what the job is, this is too casual for a job interview.

At a networking event, a good rule of thumb is to dress one level of dress higher than the typical person in the crowd. If it's a casual jeans and T-shirt event, you'll want to wear business casual such as a collared shirt and nice casual pants. The principle applies equally to men and women. If it's a black-tie event, a woman should wear her finest gown. If most of the women will be wearing a casual business suit, then wear a professional business suit.

Tip ㉝
BE WELL GROOMED.

Sometimes a networking event occurs at the end of the workday. After working the full day, running errands, maybe even taking care of the kids, you might end up a little disheveled. Take a moment for personal grooming. Men might want to shave before attending the event; women will want to double-check make-up and hair.

Again, you'll have just a few moments to make a positive impression. Don't make a bad impression. For example, if there's a stain on your shirt, change your shirt. Also consider body odor. I might not enjoy our face-to-face conversation if you've been outside, working and sweating all day. I might back away from the lingering odor of your lunchtime onion rings or garlic pizza. Brush you teeth before you go networking.

Finally, if you are a smoker, please consider the fact that your clothes may smell of cigarette smoke. This can be particularly uncomfortable to somebody who doesn't smoke or, worse yet, is allergic to cigarette smoke.

Tip ㉞
BE A RESOURCE FOR PEOPLE.

When you're a source of information for people, you're more valuable to them. If you have numerous, helpful information, or good advice to pass along, people will recognize you as a valuable resource. You'll gain respect as a useful contact or authority. People will come to you for information and you'll be more likely to be the center of attention.

Let's expand the idea of being the center of attention by thinking of a wheel. A wheel has a hub in the center, spokes radiating from the middle, and a rim around its edge. You want to be the hub. The spokes might represent professional colleagues, customers, business partners, employers, or clients. These people are all connected to you because you are in the middle. By being in the hub of information, you'll have access to all of the spokes, other people.

You can become a valuable resource when you give away the information you have. People soon see and acknowledge you for being resourceful, and eventually they'll want to return the favor by praising you and acknowledging you in the form of things like sales or referrals.

Tip ㉟
BE SOMEBODY PEOPLE ENJOY SPEAKING WITH.

We enjoy being with people we like. There's nothing complicated about that idea. It's just human nature. We don't want to put ourselves in unpleasant surroundings. We want to network with people we like. Work toward this goal in a professional networking situation by focusing on making the other person feel comfortable.

Sometimes it's frustrating to be at a networking session. We might not be in the best mood for networking. I remember being at an event where a lady was extremely agitated because she had just gotten a speeding ticket while driving to the networking mixer. She was still angry and, unfortunately, not a pleasure to speak with. Perhaps at other times in her life, she was fun to be around, but all I saw that night was her unpleasant side.

Remember, people we meet at mixers often have just one opportunity to see us in action. You don't want to create a negative image by being unpleasant. Even if you're having a bad day, do your best to be a pleasant person to speak with.

Tip 36
DETERMINE WHAT YOU WANT PEOPLE TO REMEMBER ABOUT YOU.

Always ask yourself how you want to be remembered. This reinforces our idea of being goal-centric in our networking. By working toward being remembered for something specific, you are polishing your professional image in the support of your goal.

It would be nice if people could remember everything about you. But that's an unrealistic expectation. They're more likely to remember only one thing about you. If you could leave them with only one idea, one thought, or one impression . . . what would it be?

Sometimes it's good to learn from negative examples. At a recent mixer during the self-introductions, a woman spoke about several jobs she had. One had something to do with accounting, another with sports management, and another with advertising regulations.

Was this woman an accountant for advertising regulatory agencies working with sports events planning companies? I don't know. She gave too much disparate information to remember.

Tip ㊲
SEND THANK-YOU CARDS WHEN APPROPRIATE.

It's never wrong to be polite. If you really enjoyed speaking with somebody, send him or her a thank-you card. People like being thanked. We appreciate being appreciated.

You want to be remembered. You want to stand out from the crowd. Sending a thank-you card is a strategy that can be particularly rewarding because so few people actually do it.

We live in a technologically-based world. A good portion of our daily communication is electronic. You can send your thank you via e-mail, or make a thank-you phone call, but that may not have the same powerful impact as a thank-you card.

A thank-you card can be displayed. People might stand it on their desk or pin it to their wall. This works toward your professional image by demonstrating that you are considerate, thankful, and appreciative.

Tip 38
HELP OTHERS.

I cannot stress it enough—help other people. Help people when they need help. Go out of your way to help someone. Do not hoard information or resources. By sincerely and unhesitatingly helping others, you are building a strong reputation for yourself.

When you are helpful to people, they will return the favor, often many times over. At times in client and consulting relationships, I've often provided free information or free work. Fellow consultants might say I was being overly generous or even foolish, but, more often than not, clients knew and appreciated the fact that I had gone out of my way to help them. Eventually being generous and helpful resulted in more consulting engagements for me.

Just last week, an executive recruiter called me. She was seeking an executive director for a charitable foundation. I was able to help her find an excellent candidate by recommending a friend well connected in the charitable community. Win for the person recommended. Win for the recruiter. Win for the charity. Win for me. Win. Win. Win. Win.

Tip ㊳
BE PERSISTENT, BUT NOT OBNOXIOUS.

This is particularly important in certain areas of professional networking. If you're networking for sales or to find a job, you need to be persistent.

I remember reading a newspaper article saying that it takes 7.1 calls to actually reach somebody on the phone. Even if people want to hear from you, they're often simply too busy to easily connect with. A good number of people in the United States are the victims of overflowing voice mail and e-mail in-boxes. To combat this information overflow, you need to be persistent.

But this is *not* the same thing as being obnoxious. Being persistent is continuing to follow up with somebody if you know they want to speak to you. If you know that the person doesn't want to speak to you and you still continue to attempt to contact them, that is being obnoxious.

People have often thanked me for calling multiple times. Being persistent creates opportunities. Being obnoxious kills them.

Tip 40
REINFORCE YOUR BRAND.

You're always working to create a brand for yourself. Work to reinforce your brand. If you have a logo you're proud of, display it. If you have catch phrases that are part of your marketing strategy, use them. If you can add your product brand name to what you're talking about in a general conversation, do so.

Take these steps to reinforce your brand. Part of the advantage of branding is the idea of making your brand easier to remember and making yourself more memorable.

You can leverage this strategy by using simple phrases or brand references where you can. If you're selling cruises, for example, don't say "our deluxe cruise" if the product you're pitching is the Silver-Liner Luxury Cruise Getaway. Your brand has power, but only if you work to reinforce it.

Remember that you're a brand. Your personal brand built by your image is more important than your products or your company. People are networking with *you* first.

Chapter 5

EVENT MANAGEMENT

We make a living by what we get. We make a life by what we give.

—Sir Winston Churchill

Tip ㊶
BE AT EVENTS OFTEN.

When you're a frequent attendee at a regular, reoccurring event, you'll be more effective because you're comfortable there. It's easier to speak with people you've seen and met before. Most importantly, people will be more comfortable with you. *Out of sight, out of mind* is a fairly accurate statement.

You may sell a great product that people at a given event want to buy, but they'll forget to contact you. But a new opportunity may present itself the next time they see you at an event. As soon as they see you, they remember—"I need Mark's consulting services." If Mark isn't a regular at the event, that opportunity just won't arise.

This point is especially important if you are working toward developing a long-term relationship. A long-term relationship just doesn't happen with a quick handshake and a two-minute introduction. It needs time to develop. You will be more productive in networking by being a frequent attendee to reoccurring networking events.

Tip ㊷
ATTEND THE MOST VALUABLE EVENTS.

Attend networking events that bring you the most value. If you want to meet CEOs, venture capitalists, or millionaires, you need to put yourself at the events where they're present. These might be expensive events that require travel and pricey registration fees.

If time and money are in short supply, you just need to be more creative. Here's an example of how I did this early in my career. After I returned from living and working in Europe, my goal was to leverage this experience to find a job in international business development. One event I wanted to attend was a $500 a plate awards banquet for leaders in international commerce.

At this point in my career, I could not afford this registration fee. So, I put on my tuxedo and stood outside the banquet hall, near the registration table. I got to network with the attendees. As people lingered outside the banquet hall, I spoke to them. As people were leaving, I spoke with them again.

Figure out a creative way to attend the most important events. Don't let lack of money, time, or expertise be an obstacle for you.

Tip 43
TEST DRIVE ORGANIZATIONS.

Not every organization is designed for every individual. Just like people, organizations have unique temperaments and characteristics. A particular organization may simply not be right for you.

It may be overly bureaucratic or inflexible. Its mixers may be too far away. It may have a vision not in line with your core competency. There can be a myriad of reasons why the organization doesn't meet your needs. That's OK. When you test-drive organizations, you can learn which ones fit and which ones don't.

Most organizations have guest policies. They allow and even encourage you to try out their organization. They want to see if you're the right fit. They generally won't make you join immediately.

If you do attend some meetings as a guest and enjoy the organization, they might ask you to join and pay membership dues. This is only reasonable. Organizations have operational costs associated with networking mixers.

Tip ㊹
VOLUNTEER AT ORGANIZATIONS YOU LIKE.

If you truly like an organization, becoming a volunteer in that organization can give you greater access to events and event information. You might gain insight into event planning that typical members don't have.

For example, when you volunteer, you'll know about the programs and events that are planned as well as events that were rejected. When you help plan networking events, you'll have access to information that the general members might not have access to.

Suppose that, as a member of a financial planning organization, you are tasked with managing a financial planning trade show with several recognized professionals speaking or performing workshops. You'll have personal access to these people because you'll need to speak to them to plan the event.

Also, as a leader in the organization, you're demonstrating commitment and leadership skills. As people see you becoming more involved, they'll have greater respect for you and become more comfortable working with you.

Tip 45
PRE-REGISTER FOR EVENTS.

Take the time and extra effort to pre-register for events. The organizers of the event and the leaders of the sponsoring organization will notice your consideration and professionalism.

Generally, established mixer events have a registration process. I've registered for events via fax, e-mail, mail, and website registration.

There are several advantages to pre-registering. First, when you have the event on your calendar, you can more effectively budget your time. Second, if there are supporting messages such as speaker biographies, parking instructions, or venue changes, they can be more easily communicated to you.

Also, please realize that *not* pre-registering has significant disadvantages. I've been at events where at-the-door registrants had to be accommodated at the last minute and seated at an extra table set-up by the event manager. If you didn't pre-register, the event planner will know it. *You* are the person that made them do extra, last minute work. You're not making a positive impression.

Tip ㊻
BE THE FIRST ONE AT THE EVENT.

The advantages of this tip should be obvious. If you're the first one to arrive, then you'll have greater opportunity to speak with more people. Maximize your time at the event by being the first one there.

Why not make the most of the event? If you're the first one there, you can meet more people. You probably had to rearrange your schedule and possibly pay a registration fee to attend. When you're the first one there, you can maximize your time and money.

Being the first one there can also lead to special access to information. Depending on the event, the location and the sponsoring organization, the event team might be still in set-up mode at the scheduled start of the event. This might provide you insider access. Event planners are more flexible with information and conversation because there are fewer people that need their attention before the majority of the participants arrive.

Tip 47
BE THE LAST ONE TO LEAVE THE EVENT.

This is really the same as the previous tip, but in reverse. When you're the last one to leave, you not only have the opportunity to meet more people, but you can also follow up with people before they leave. This gives you, in effect, two good first impressions.

Sometimes you'll be able to talk with someone at the beginning of a networking mixer. You've planted a seed at the beginning of the meeting. At the end of the meeting, you can revisit that idea. The person you spoke to may have taken time during the meeting to ponder your idea, suggestion, or request and be able to give you some immediate feedback.

I've experienced this several times. An initial comment at the beginning of a networking mixer—"I don't think that's a good idea"—evolves into "Actually, I think we can do that," by the end of the evening.

By staying until the very end of networking events, you maximize your opportunities.

Tip ⑱
BE FLEXIBLE WITH TIME COMMITMENTS AFTER AN EVENT.

When you're flexible with your time commitments after the scheduled end of the event, you'll be able to continue networking with any great people you met that night. Sometimes you'll make a true connection with someone and you'll want to continue speaking with them.

For example, I've attended networking events and been involved in intriguing conversations with people. After the event, we moved to a local bar and went on with the conversation.

You can, of course, set a time when you can meet again and renew your conversation. But, by immediately continuing the conversation, you can more effectively address any opportunities that develop between you and your conversational partner.

There are other benefits as well. In a one-on-one conversation, after the event, there is less general distraction. Also, the person will see that you have enough interest in them to meet with them immediately.

Tip ㊾
WORK TO PRE-QUALIFY EVENTS.

Your time is valuable. It's useful to maximize your networking productivity with a pre-qualification process designed to meet your networking strategy. By knowing the basics of the event, you can evaluate the worthiness of the event.

When you know the purpose of the event, its cost, its location, and the number of attendees, you can decide if it meets your needs. Also consider traveling time, such as drive time for local events.

I live in the greater Los Angeles area. Depending on the specific location of a networking event and traffic congestion on the freeways, the drive time might be as long as three hours. In this scenario, an event attended by only six people might not qualify as a rewarding event. If, however, these people were all CEOs of their own firms, then perhaps it would be a good event.

Without the proper information about the basics of the event, you'll be unable to make an informed decision about participating.

Tip 50
TARGET CUSTOMER-RICH MEETINGS.

Determine where your target customers might be and go there yourself. If you're selling something (including yourself if you're on a job search), then you need to be where your customers are.

If you're a marketing person and want to learn about marketing, then certainly it makes sense to attend marketing seminars, trade shows, and workshops. If you're a marketing person trying to market a product, marketing-centric events are not your best target.

Imagine that you're a wedding planner trying to promote your business. You should attend bridal shows. That type of networking opportunity is obvious. Should you attend events of hospitality management organizations? You might think that you shouldn't because you don't manage a hotel, but keep in mind that these people will be hosting wedding rehearsal dinners and receptions. Those hotel and convention center managers are potential customers, too.

When you attend events that are a likely good source of consumers, clients, and potential leads, you can be a more effective networker.

TO LEARN MORE

To learn more about Mark Mikelat and his speaking and training engagements, or to learn more about his core Aspirations Message, please contact:

Mark Mikelat
PO Box 14885
Long Beach, CA 90803

mark@buildingaspirations.com

Buildingaspirations.com

People interested in networking have also been interested in some of the following programs:

Working Your Network: How to *Mind* for Gold

Aspirations Career Planning: Your Dream Career Roadmap

Exciting Excitement: Using Excitement for Greater Effectiveness

ABOUT THE AUTHOR

Mark Mikelat has always been dedicated to community service. He has cleaned beaches, repaired houses, delivered food, donated blood and clothes. In recognition of his dedication to community service, the German Television Radio ZDF 10, Charter News, and eNews have all interviewed him.

Mark holds a Master of International Business Administration degree from Pepperdine University and the European Business School, a program which included curricula in the United States, Spain, France, Germany, and Switzerland. He was graduated summa cum laude from Arizona State University with a Bachelor of Science degree in Computer Information Systems.

Currently he is an adjunct faculty member at Long Beach City College, where he teaches several classes in the international business department. Mark is also a trustee emeritus of the Leadership Foundation of Delta Sigma Pi, a college scholarship and leadership training association for business students. He works tirelessly to inspire people with the message of Aspirations at keynote speeches and seminars.